ADVANCE PRAISE FOR *MY GRIEF, T.*

"Sanna Wani's *My Grief, the Sun* makes such a convincing case for astonishment as a way of life. Each poem enveloped me with so much tenderness it was as if *I* were the sun! The theological music that courses throughout the book was not a narrowing toward some esoteric knowledge but rather an opening toward a collective sense of enmeshment with the inscrutable world. This book is a necessary reminder that 'there is something inside / [us] that says live.' *My Grief, the Sun* is a wonder and a delight."
— Billy-Ray Belcourt, author of *This Wound Is a World* and *NDN Coping Mechanisms*

"I read Sanna Wani's *My Grief, the Sun* with a highlighter in my hand, and by the time I was done, it was nearly out of ink. I could not stop loving lines, wanting to be sure I remembered them always. They progress with such sureness into marvelous and unexpected directions: 'God climbs so many trees. Religion is a ladder. We are meant to help Him down.' Over and over, Wani practices the act of artful surrender to each poem's strange, budding logic. That she can do so with such apparent ease is astonishing. That we get to witness the places her gorgeous poems take her is a profound gift. I'm wonderstruck."
— Heather Christle, author of *Heliopause* and *The Trees The Trees*

"Mapping us through time, space, and geography, Sanna Wani's debut collection *My Grief, the Sun* spins a web of various griefs and loves. As visual as it is lyrical, Wani announces herself as a poet who pushes the experimentation of form forward, taking bold risks and literally reinventing the way that we see language. 'A mosque is always directed toward Mecca. A dome does not have orientation unless it is toward the sky,' Wani writes, and pointing her eyes to the sky, and with incredible vision, makes even the tiniest detail visible."
— Fatimah Asghar, author of *If They Come for Us*

MY GRIEF, THE SUN

poems

Sanna Wani

ANANSI

Published in Canada in 2022 and the USA in 2022 by House of Anansi
Press Inc.
www.houseofanansi.com

House of Anansi Press is committed to protecting our natural
environment. This book is made of material from well-managed
FSC®-certified forests, recycled materials, and other controlled sources.

House of Anansi Press is a Global Certified Accessible™ (GCA by Benetech)
publisher. The ebook version of this book meets stringent accessibility
standards and is available to students and readers with print disabilities.

26 25 24 23 22   1 2 3 4 5

Library and Archives Canada Cataloguing in Publication

Title: My grief, the sun : poems / Sanna Wani.
Names: Wani, Sanna, author.
Identifiers: Canadiana (print) 2021037554X |
Canadiana (ebook) 20210379456 | ISBN 9781487010843 (softcover) |
ISBN 9781487010850 (EPUB)
Classification: LCC PS8645.A55 M9 2022 | DDC C811/.6—dc23

Cover design: Alysia Shewchuk
Text design: Laura Brady
Typesetting: Laura Brady and Marijke Friesen

*House of Anansi Press respectfully acknowledges that the land on which
we operate is the Traditional Territory of many Nations, including the
Anishinabeg, the Wendat, and the Haudenosaunee. It is also the Treaty Lands
of the Mississaugas of the Credit.*

Canada Council   Conseil des Arts
for the Arts   du Canada

ONTARIO ARTS COUNCIL
CONSEIL DES ARTS DE L'ONTARIO
an Ontario government agency
un organisme du gouvernement de l'Ontario

With the participation of the Government of Canada
Avec la participation du gouvernement du Canada | Canadä

*We acknowledge for their financial support of our publishing program the Canada
Council for the Arts, the Ontario Arts Council, and the Government of Canada.*

for you

CONTENTS

I.

Dorsal   3

Masha'Allah   5
Today and Every Day, Without You   6
Memory Is Sleeping   8
Bilabial   9
How Many Languages Make a Tongue?   11
Tragedy   12
Schizotheism   13
Princess Mononoke (1997)
    I. Ashitaka and the Forest Spirit   15
    II. San and Moro   16
    III. Yakul and Ashitaka   17
Meditation   18
Between Spring Equinox and Summer Solstice, Tonight   20
Pendulum   21
Sing   22

II. Forming Glory

Relief   25

morphology

I would rather like to go back again / Dome of Rock   28
A footprint is shown / Two ascensions   29
Spirit is not inheritance / Exegesis then   30
Testimony / Discipline was proud   31
Start talking about God's form then / But how does
God look in His most beautiful form?   32
Theologians are weavers / All of this is exegesis   33

doxology

Where is the key for our understanding? /
We look in vain for any hint of God's footprint   36
God is the Exalted and Absolute Other /
Transcendence may look etiolated   37
Creation / Speculation   38
Do not believe in God / God as a radiant body   39
What does God think of beauty? /
Hunger and materiality   40
Enthusiasm finds parallels /
Parallel is alone at the end of the line   41

III.

Reaching   45

My Grief, the Sun   47
Who Is the Sun, Asking for Sleep?   49
Good Morning, the Sun in October   50
Crayfish Watch the Moon Fall   51
I Am Off to Meet the Himalayas   53
A Rose Is a Mouth with No Teeth   55
We Don't Want to Love People So Different from Us   56
The Very Slow Steps Toward You   57
I Am Listening to the Doves Coo   58
We Are Whispering in the Dark   59
Why I Pray   60
Your Departure, a Loneliness   62
I Remember an Incident Where My Mother Begs Me   64
Children Cackle like a Band of Hyenas   66
Asifa   67
Mind's Eye   69

IV. Distances

Direction   73

winter

    Tomorrow is a place   78
    Each step, a hope   79
    A place I call my hands   80
    Here is the world   81

spring

    Sorrow is a promise   84
    My worry, a callous   85
    My anger was made   86
    There is only so much   87

summer

    Joy is a promise   90
    That moth, breathing   91
    There is a wish   92
    There is still someone   93

fall

Even the wood whispers   96
Another word for this place   97
A lilac, or lily   98
I follow a song   99

Notes   101
Acknowledgements   105

I.

s singing. I
y drop. Yes, me
warmth of your back. I
Come closer. Let me try
in. Let me. Again, please. And
gain. And again. Again. I'm
lowing. The rain is singing. I love
ou. Yes, every, drop. Yes, me too.
The warmth of your back. I could.
Come closer. Let me try again. Let
me. Again, please. And again. And
again. Again. I'm glowing. The rain
is singing. I love you. Yes, every
drop. Yes, me too. The warmth of
your back. I could. Come closer.
Let me try again. Let me. Again,
please. And again. And again.
Again. I'm glowing. The rain is
singing. I love you. Yes, every
drop. Yes, me too. The warmth of
your back. I could. Come closer.
Let me try again. Let me. Again,
please. And again. And again.
Again. I'm glowing. The rain is
singing. I love you. Yes, every
drop. Yes, me too. The warmth of
your back. I could. Come closer.
Let me try again. Let me. Again,
please. And again. And again.
Again. I'm glowing. The rain is
singing. I love you. Yes, every
drop. Yes, me too. the warmth of
I could. Come closer.
again. Let me. Again,
nd again. And again.
m glowing. The rain is
I love you. Yes, every
Yes, me too. The warmth of

your back
Let me try ag
please. And ag
Again. I'm glowing.
singing. I love you. Yes, e
drop. Yes, me too. The warmth
your back. I could. Come close
Let me try again. Let me. Again,
please. And again. And again.
Again. I'm glowing. The rain is
singing. I love you. Yes, every
drop. Yes, me too. The warmth of
your back. I could. Come closer.
Let me try again. Let me. Again,
please. And again. And again.
Again. I'm glowing. The rain is
singing. I love you. Yes, every
drop. Yes, me too. The warmth of
your back. I could. Come closer.
Let me try again. Let me. Again,
please. And again. And again.
Again. I'm glowing. The rain is
singing. I love you. Yes, every
drop. Yes, me too. The warmth of
your back. I could. Come closer.
Let me try again. Let me. Again,
please. And again. And again.
Again. I'm glowing. The rain is
singing. I love you. Yes, every
drop. Yes, me too. the warmth of
your back. I could. Come clos
Let me try again. Let me. Ag
please. And again. And a
Again. I'm glowing. The r
singing. I love you. Yes
drop. Yes, me too. The w
your back. I could. Com
Let me try again. Let me

DORSAL, *after Mitski*

[3]

I write simply so that my friends love me very much
and that those who love me very much love me more.

—Gabriel García Márquez

MASHA'ALLAH

after Danusha Laméris

I am eager for any mouth to open
that soft word, "what God wills."
Masha'Allah your hands are so gentle.
The baby is so happy, masha'Allah.
Masha'Allah we all have enough to eat.

So much joy I've carried has soured
easily as plums under nobody's eyes.

Every language must have this seal.
A word to protect our breath
from the world's unruly hands,
luck's staggering gait.

Our children have grown up to be so kind, masha'Allah.
Masha'Allah the birds are singing in the fields again.
Masha'Allah the rice is alive in the grove.

How lightly we learn to hold each blessing,
as if it were the wind, trembling at an unlocked door.
And still we wait for it, ceaselessly, the way a child would,
patience pouring into each word, from one mouth to the next.

TODAY AND EVERY DAY, WITHOUT YOU

> *I don't care*
> *about the flowers, which I merely invented*
> *to give myself another reason to address you.*
> — Aleksandar Ristović

is long   and sharp   tastes
like milk   and salt   a teacup where
you sat   like so many trees   is now
dry   we drink   like tired fossils
from the rock   of our want   from the dregs

of green   and pink flowers   hungry
for the sun like   the roses in the garden
or the dream I had   where you became
the sky   where I met you   in the un-
hurried blue of an afternoon daisy

who stands to greet me   the sun
the breeze sliding down the letter h
until I am home   waiting for your call
my mother watching the water sit still in
the garden   light bouncing   continually
through our hands   the marble   of the door
bright bronze and broken   o hungry flowers

I am trying   to show you how quiet the slope
of my desire sits on the hillside endless
buried there you are in every beautiful thing
wearing the light again I am watching
the trees again the sky is calling

for quiet the morning   like everyone's eyes   the door
shut tight only the daisies   unfurling watching   as I leave

MEMORY IS SLEEPING

Sometimes remembering refuses us. Sometimes I'm
a shoreline the water of memory drags its palm across.
— Billy-Ray Belcourt

In a daisy field. In a garden. In a graveyard, in the sun,
its valley. In the sound of nothing. Your mother and father,
two trees in the distance. In the distance. In the sound of the whistle,
someone banishing you again. A hand in the distance, a greeting.

In a greeting, a question. How old are you? Six? Seventeen?
In your body, ageing, an immediacy. In a flower, a new arm.
Eat the apple. Your lips redden. The person you were, you
are always becoming. Their breath spilling over your neck.

A breath, a shore, a whistle, a knife. Where is the wind?
In love, the wounds you tend. A wound, a door, a lake, a fence.
Whatever is perpendicular to your becoming. Time is a terrible statue.
The tide will eat its skin. To prevent heartbreak, practise disappearing.

All the eels are missing. You are an expert in missing. A mouth,
a lock, a gate, a key. Open your mouth and throw the word *yet*
into the river. Into the river, your face leaking glass. A face,
a flood, a crystal, a dove. Someday, you will be in love again.

The sun, a wound on your windowsill. Light falls
on your dreams. It sounds like someone knocking.

BILABIAL

after Myung Mi Kim

murmur/murmured/murmuring
to separate the fire from the crackle

meander/meandered/meandering
to find money on the sidewalk

mourn/mourned/mourning
to drain the ocean from one shell

marble/marbled/marbling
to make a map, to mould

mellow/mellowed/mellowing
to loosen colour, to fart

melody/melodic/melodies
to remember, to bloom

morning/mornings/mourner
to alert the sun, to set a reminder

melancholy/melancholia
to dismember a rock, to disavow

murder/murdered/murdering
to empty the fridge, to discard spoiled meat

momentum/momentous/momentary
to lock eyes with motion, to croon

magnify/magnificent/magnetic
to tilt the bone, to tire out an edge

HOW MANY LANGUAGES MAKE A TONGUE?

after Yoko Tawada

~~No, let me ask again.~~

Where does the word live?

~~Yes, I guess nowhere is not wrong.~~

Nothing asks for wrongness.

~~Yes, nothing asks to be spoken.~~

But we call for it anyway.

~~No, no one is named your kin.~~

But you call for them anyway.

~~Just try to hear this.~~

Here, this.

~~This heat is spreading quickly.~~

This heat is spreading.

~~Quickly.~~

Did you catch it?

TRAGEDY

after Alejandra Pizarnik

Wall broken into window.
I ask, *Where can I bury my knife?*
Mourning my open shoulder.

Who are the mountain goats?
Do they exist? Where have you seen them?
Who is climbing the steep today?

What a terrible song, this hoofed wind.
What a terrible song, the begging of my body.
I am the knife. I am the knife. I am the knife.

A goat is waiting at the foot of the slope.
A sycamore tree by the peak. The old world
is a ghost; this valley, a coliseum.

Mountain goats sleep on their knees.
Someone is singing on the steep.
The echo carries; the snow weeps.

Allah:
There you are, behind this heavy wall.
There you are, singing by the peak.
There you are; the wound, the warning.

What am I, then? The breach?

SCHIZOTHEISM

Fajr

Allah grew up an orphan. Space was a lofty sea and Allah fell asleep on
a spinning disk then woke up inside a star, hands already busy, hands
already turning hydrogen to hexagons. Allah lives inside a quark. Tiny
and tampering with the incessant ticking inside us, pulling on a pair of
reading glasses because Their eyes get tired of looking at the small things
too. Allah picked a spot to stand steady in the darkness. Balanced out
the bend of orbits — for your sake and mine — and that's some kind of
loyalty, isn't it?

Zuhr

Allah lingers. Next to me on a bus at 7 p.m., then smoking a cigarette
under the willow trees when there is nothing in the sky but thunder.
Allah never stops dancing. Never stops spinning, never stops laughing
when They are drunk with movement and other fizzy drinks, says
it might be the only real passion They have. I asked Them once, *Is
your universe expanding?* and They answered hastily, *I'm searching for
Something More — please don't worry — I'm just flushing out my father —*

Allah wants to spread Their hands so far apart wings sprout from Their
cracked nails.

Asr

Allah has a hard time touching anything that isn't Their Infinite Self. So the burns that ache are sometimes by accident but not always. No, Allah is not *lonely*. Obviously Allah is not lonely — how could you ask that? Allah is the only thing inherent to anything — the only core to stand on — how could you ask if They were —

Maghrib

Oh. Allah hid this from me. Never lied, but omission is a talent and my empathy has always been an inconvenience. Allah has never found a parent. No, never learned a name other than Their own, has been pressing on the lines trying to undo time but time is a little god of her own. A begetter of wild horses and even my Allah can't tame her.

Isha

I wonder what became of my Allah, after that one time They came to me in a dream and whispered, *Are you me or am I you?*

PRINCESS MONONOKE (1997)

for Terry

I. Ashitaka and the Forest Spirit

power / noun (from Latin *posse*, "to be able")

Something is strange in the forest. Something is coming. Something is coming closer.

Under your eyes is the sound of the river we crossed together. There is the light, its pronounced slant. Every day, I wait for you on the other side.

Death is not what you should fear. Death is a mercy. Death is relief for those of us who have trespassed where the light can follow.

A demon is slick as oil. When your spirit is broken, it shows on your skin. Violet violation. Hatred undoes your shadow.

The wound awoke near silence. Was power the place or the god? I did not ask to heal then I did. You made a promise to die and you kept it.

Night extends your neck. You reached for the moon, turned to look back. You knew she had come to kill you. You did not look away. The gun sprouted. I was a witness. This was how deeply you could reach into something dead and still pull out more life.

You cannot alter your fate but you can rise to meet it if you choose. I rose. I met Fate, a poison in the forest, and asked, *What will it take to start again? Where do I need to go?*

Who wants to rule this world? Who is ready for the hunt? What is the difference between hunger and war? Eating and surviving?

Power hunts power. Every step, a giant silence. Underwater, you were old again. Out of my wound, you drank. What was untouched by ego? I dreamt of an immense yellow light. I dreamt nothing was over as long as we were alive.

II. San and Moro

vulnerable / adjective (from Latin *vulnerare*, "to wound")

O nameless god, the
mountains are dying.
The trees cry out as they
die but humans cannot
hear them. There is a
fire in this land that will
burn and burn until
nothing is left.

Mother, I hate the smell
of my skin. I hate the
way it stretches toward
each light. There is
something inside me
that says *live* so I must.
There is something
inside me that says *try*
and I cannot stop.

*Pour water over each
wound.* What about the
wound inside me, the
wound I was born into?
Where do I pour when I
am the wound? I am
what wounds me.

I will not sit and watch
our home be destroyed.
I have no need for love.
I have no need for
memory. Grief eats from
my soul, Mother, the
one everyone says
you stole.

I begged the boar god
to stop running. But the
corpses of his warriors
gathered around him.
There was nothing that
could halt this haunting.
There is no one who
does not mourn
recklessly, especially
not a god.

He gives me a necklace
that says, *Do not forget.*
The glint of his tears.
Memory slips outside
the body. We mimic the
gods to feel like them.
I carry your wounds
because I want to
remember you.

Between night and day,
life and death are alone
together. This is where
you could kill a god.
This is when you could
heal the forest, once
and for all.

Human hands must
return what they take.
If this is what it takes to
heal the Forest Spirit,
Mother, then I must
acknowledge my skin.
I must acknowledge
my hands.

What is life itself can
never die. I do not
forgive. I carry voices,
a promise. To live,
to honour sacrifice.
We pass on a name, a
story. *Our god fell.* And
everything he fell into
came back to life.

III. Yakul and Ashitaka

carry / verb (from Latin *currere*, "to run")

I do not remember a moment when I was not by your side. I do not put much weight in memory but trust is balance. Your presence, a patience pressed into my chest.

She calls me this word, *wise*. What does it mean? I am still waiting for you to wake up. She is still waiting for me to leave without you.

Death is simple. It is not like hate. It does not linger. Grief and I face the dawn he disappears into. Then we turn to face the sun.

Something is wrong. We have to leave. Your face is different now. You only look honestly at me.

We wade into the water together. You feed me first. This is how it has always been. You are my friend.

There is a way the grass waves during goodbyes. As if even the wind knows it is time to part. We are finally ready to go.

She says to me, *You're free. You can go now.* You were sleeping. I can tell, these days, even your dreams are tiring.

The one you all call *god* is my kin. His fur is bright. This is the nature of blood. But I know better than to intrude on someone else's home. I know better than to try and claim a god.

You are my kin. Before blood, I am your family. Companionship means *who runs together* and I run with you. Wherever we go, love will follow.

MEDITATION

after Aisha Sasha John

Today I drew a heart between my left middle and index finger.
I drew a star between the middle and the ring and then I remembered:

> I have a vein in that finger that goes directly to my heart.
> Is there any part of me that doesn't go directly to my heart?

My jaw is aching. A friend I haven't spoken to in years says, *Soften
your jaw.* That yoga video I watch on really bad days, *Soften your gaze.*

> Or did I get them mixed up again?
> Inside my head, there is a big, big ocean.

Gentle is where the water is ankle high and warm, where the water is
warm even when the sun disappears and the sun disappears. Often,

> I find softness is a moon in my mouth melting.
> The eyes of the kitten I wait for each morning

are amber. I wait with milk and bones. I kneel. I put whatever is in my hands
on the ground and whatever is alive nestles between my feet. My heart breaks.

Once someone touched my jaw so softly I cried.
Once someone held my hand so lightly I wept —

Oh, light, what are you doing here? How did you get inside this poem?
Listen, light, once I put an egg in the mouth of a golden retriever.

His fur glowed warm in the sun. Cesium is the softest of all
metals, not gold. If I put a stone in my mouth, will it melt?

Gold is not poison. A river is not alive but is soft. The rock it touches too.
River is my word for vein. *Rock* for what I offer you, like this poem.

BETWEEN SPRING EQUINOX AND SUMMER SOLSTICE, TONIGHT

after Emily Jungmin Yoon

I read a Shahid poem with the line,
      "The world is full of paper,"
      and I am writing.

Tonight I have been.
      Tonight I have enough paper
      for three letters and no ink.

I think about the word *bahar* in Urdu.
      It means *heavy*. It means *outside*.
      It means *to carry*. To pride.

Tonight we carry paper.
      Tonight we stack the hours
      word by word. The full face

of the moon as open as the page.
      Someone says *Ishmael* and your books
      whisper with light. My wrist as loose

as the door. My wrist, the canon
      of a song. *Bahar*, I write. *It's spring.*
      We sleep. It's warm outside.

PENDULUM

for Max

Yes, we are ringed by funny light.

No, the flowers are not timid.

Yes, our haloes can sing.

No, our longing is not bothered.

Yes, our hands are a cure.

No, we don't untangle what we speak.

Yes, there is a horizon to my desire.

No, I am not a sun.

Yes, our grief melts.

No, it does not sour.

Yes, a dream can fly.

No, it will not wait for anyone.

Yes, we sigh in unison.

No, the birds are not listening.

Yes, someone is singing.

No, I am not the song.

SING

after Juan Felipe Herrera

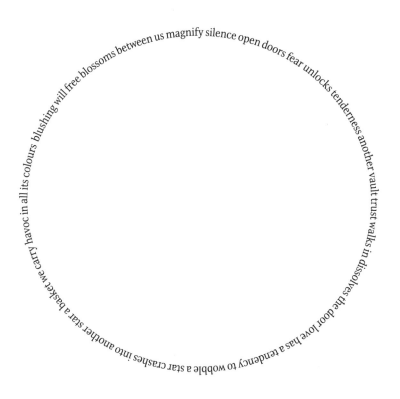

blushing will free blossoms between us magnify silence open doors fear unlocks tenderness another vault trust walks in dissolves the door love has a tendency to wobble a star crashes into another star a basket we carry havoc in all its colours

II.
Forming Glory

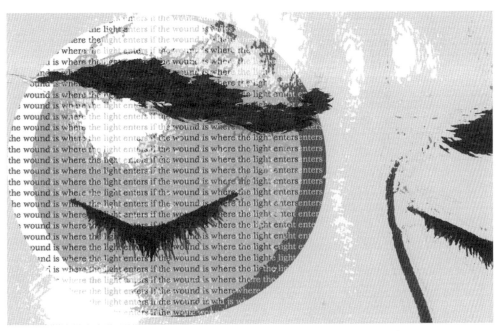

RELIEF, *after Rumi*

morphology
/ mɔrˈfɑlədʒi /

noun

a study in the form of language

Essentially, language represents a wound for me.

—M. NourbeSe Philip

I WOULD RATHER LIKE TO GO BACK AGAIN Once to the basis on which theology was built. Once to where movement drew strength. Once to when the Qur'an was the Prophet's mouth. Once to the Hadith, which was a descent of mouths. Once to silence, its assent, an ushering. Once to tradition, its notorious elusive. Once to God's geography, a dome, a rock. Once to some kind of chronology, its pulsating measure. Once to a conclusion built on good chance. To an encounter built on good faith. Once to the enumerated God. The God of motivation.

DOME OF ROCK The edifice is crucial. Trace out the earliest pattern. Architecture is meaning and meaning loses all direction. It was not a mosque. It was not meant to be. A mosque is always directed toward Mecca. A dome does not have orientation unless it is toward the sky.

A FOOTPRINT IS SHOWN Inside, a visitor is told, *Prophet Muhammad ascended from that spot.* Nocturnal journey. Heaven under Gabriel's guidance. This is an old tradition. We possess through forgotten evidence. That some people believe in God leaves a mark on the rock. Between the terrestrial and the paradisal was God. It was from the rock. Who had returned again? To Heaven.

TWO ASCENSIONS To Heaven and a chosen person. The motive is much older. God sitting on a throne. God drawing near. God whispering. How the Prophet knew God was a friend was with a hand. The word masih is derived from Aramaic. *With a hand.* But masaha in Arabic is different. *To wipe a person's head, to pass a hand over.* Someone has been touched. God is passing over.

SPIRIT IS NOT INHERITANCE Islam expanded, unprecedented. From East to West, then back again. Morality shifted form. Revelation needs a body. Misgiving gains ground, then loses it. Wander, then lose your feet. Maybe this is what happened to God.

EXEGESIS THEN was the vehicle of thought. Interpretation is intimacy. What was the first word spoken? Contradiction was unthinkable. The perennial, the past, the peninsula. Everything could be early. The historian was left with the task. *Find out what is behind those words.* The hidden was still left open.

TESTIMONY Samad means God *as He neither eats nor drinks*. Theodore of Upper Mesopotamia translated Samad into Greek as sphuropektos. *Hammered together, closely united.* Nicetas of Byzantium later used holosphuros instead. *Entirely chased in metal, a completely round thing.*

DISCIPLINE WAS PROUD of having overcome milieu. But in the capital, it did not fare well. It became the victim of its own terminology. It insisted on calling God a body so it was buried. It insisted God had no form so it disappeared.

START TALKING ABOUT GOD'S FORM THEN God visited the Prophet at night in His most beautiful form. He put His hand between the Prophet's shoulder blades. A coolness he fell through. The other side was neither Heaven nor Hell. This gesture was a gift. A seed is a kind of stone. Belief is touch. This is the only theological proof.

BUT HOW DOES GOD LOOK IN HIS MOST BEAUTIFUL FORM? Some say He has exuberant hair, like a thousand wings. Everyone agrees He has no beard. Some call Him the oldest day. This is an awareness of time. If you gather God from the length of your life, you're lucky if you can put together one day.

THEOLOGIANS ARE WEAVERS On the rock, there are four letters. Hapax legomenon. Any assertion of meaning is strange and striking. You ask, *What does a word really mean in the Qur'an?* when you should ask, *What increases our bewilderment?* There is no answer for how the word was first understood. We only have sounds left over, and a memory in the air around them.

ALL OF THIS IS EXEGESIS because faith is complex geology. Arabic was how the Prophet spoke. But language is not made of time. Neither is God. So how do we sing elegies? Someone thought God needed a mirror. A reflection to consider. What can we conclude about sight? The power to create? We slipped out of God's hand. God's hand, out of light.

doxology
/dɒkˈsɒlədʒi/

noun

a study in the glory of language

Have wings that feared
ever touched the Sun?

— Rabia of Basra

WHERE IS THE KEY FOR OUR UNDERSTANDING? Look at the lock. No one can prove tradition. Nothing can be located, not even the spot from where God left the earth. Everyone is always competing to be the most sacred. This is how we think of the early. Everything is always moving. The idea of You was not new. But it was arriving someplace it had not been, like inside us. Where it could strike root. Where it could blossom.

WE LOOK IN VAIN FOR ANY HINT OF GOD'S FOOTPRINT It would have folklore. A path. We want proof of the imperial self and God wants to breathe. Look in either direction. The day is an orientation of light. The ocean, an endless symmetry. I want a God who says, *I want nothing from you.* I want to prove the self is hollow. We love a kind of silence. An absence we extend.

GOD IS THE EXALTED AND ABSOLUTE OTHER All the books agree. But history is not a book. It is true for a long time, then dust. Find God where He is. He used our terminology to escape attention. God climbs so many trees. Religion is a ladder. We are meant to help Him down.

TRANSCENDENCE MAY LOOK ETIOLATED but let's promise you can visit Him at least once in your dreams. Of course it is not desirable to enter Paradise immediately. There is so much more to see. God's glory spills over the night, as brilliant and patient as the moon.

CREATION God does not touch matter. When He creates, He calls. He uses His own name. This name is not chosen. God transforms whatever is inherent as similar. This is identity, not the propertied self. Under this aspect, creation unfolds. At the end of each day, God puts us back together again.

SPECULATION Near God's secret name, there is a giant Calotropis. Honesty offers wings. God's name took flight, then settled, crooked, on the lip of God's crown.

DO NOT BELIEVE IN GOD is a phrase we know already. Denial is solid. Solid is sublime. Tendency is the process and the process loses all material. Craft is flesh and blood. Calligraphy replaces the corporeal. Imagine these letters are made of light and they are. Imagine God is luminous and God is luminous.

GOD AS A RADIANT BODY A crystal, a pearl, a silver ingot.

WHAT DOES GOD THINK OF BEAUTY? God was not astonished to find God described. He is amused at our musings. Beauty fractures form. It is no wonder we are confused.

HUNGER AND MATERIALITY sit side by side, bumping shoulders. They never completely agree. How does God sit? What are His bones made of? Does He glow? Paradise can stretch its feet to earth. Mount Zion touches the sky. But God is a speck in the wind. All of God's monuments and the key is still missing. We long for You so badly. We have been looking for You for so long.

ENTHUSIASM FINDS PARALLELS but do not be blind to difference. There is no imitating glory. Just a forked line between where we dream and where we die. Where the mystics thought God to be invisible, even the angels did not see Him. When epiphanies take place in fire, even His light cannot enter us.

PARALLEL IS ALONE AT THE END OF THE LINE and what have we gathered? Strokes of chronology and geology. Maps and nests of time. What will we look for today? The spider and the fish. We must be patient. God was old at the edge of a still lake, singing a beloved song. You might not make out the words but you can hear a melody. God, whose feathers are as black as the raven. God, who is the song.

III.

REACHING, *after Anne Carson*

I love the sun for worshipping no one.
I love the sun for showing up every day.

—Alex Dimitrov

I am on my way to see you. It has almost been four years since you've been gone and four is my favourite number. It also means death in languages I don't know but meaning is from wherever meaning is from. Death can be one or it can be many — it doesn't make a difference when it has almost been four years. You've been gone and the barley behind your grave has grown golden. The sun is so bright on our drive over that I have to pull the visor down and my mother remarks that my mouth looks like it's on fire.

I'll admit it. I have not visited you in months. I have already counted four planes passing over us. I ask, "Who is us?" like, "Is she still here?" I told my brother once that I could not feel you here to begin with. He disagrees. He says, "I put her here — I lowered her into this ground — I saw her face for the last time — here." I understand but I don't. Women are not allowed to touch graves apparently. It was almost heresy that we showed up to the burial at all. My mother, my sister, my aunts and cousins, a few hundred feet away, watching a crowd of men lower you into the ground. I stood so still I wondered if anyone could see me. Then I felt a terrible guilt because who was I to be seen here?

Today I am wearing your ring and standing as close to your grave as I want, and it is almost four years later, which is very close. I wear your ring every day and I feel strange without it but I still don't call it mine. I think I feel similarly about your loss. I stare at grief and try to call it mine, then feel terrible, then selfish. I stare at your grave and try to pray, then wonder what kind of grief prayer is.

Maybe I should just tell you this. Your son will be getting on a flight tomorrow to go back to an island. He tries his best not to feel lonely without you and I am always, stupidly, trying to love him for you. It is always wrong but never is. I am wearing a necklace your husband gave me for my twenty-first birthday. He emptied your drawers within a week of your passing but hasn't moved your purse from its place on the shelf since the day we took you to the hospital. I am trying to love them both but I am very bad at it. I am trying to use my whole heart but I am very bad at that too. I wrote this after all. Long-winded, long, winding way of using almost blinding sunsets and grown golden barley just to say, *I think of you so often.* We miss you so much.

WHO IS THE SUN, ASKING FOR SLEEP?

Or just cold air. I know there was a time I chose not to speak for four days and my voice felt like a heavy roach after. Part of having a body means whatever can be felt can be forgotten. Forgetting is like sleep, like water. Heavy wet brain. Clear swollen dreams. It is some kind of relief, I guess, that whatever I am will be gone one day. I know several names for several types of wind. *Mistral* and *monsoon*. Bodies, in *resonance* or *inflammation*. But I don't pretend to understand how wind works. I know I can feel it on my face. I know I will forget.

So I continue running. Waiting. Opening all the windows. In the morning, I am not this harsh. But grief compels me, maybe even more than sleep. I am waiting for something to last. I know nothing will. But I am waiting for mornings that do not end or maybe they do but *end* is not the right word at all. I would call these mornings *georgic* or *fraying*. The spinning, the earth breathing. Every four days, I learn how to speak again. I remember the spin is slowing. The days growing longer.

GOOD MORNING, THE SUN IN OCTOBER

makes the leaves look like they have been spun out of gold
and there are several kinds of hickory trees growing outside
my window. The bitternut is my favourite because from
far away the leaves look like moss and up close they look
like scales. When autumn light bleeds new colours into things,
or out of them, a garden snake will take a nap on the warm wood
of a branch and wake up as a frond and ask, "When did I turn to gold?"

But remember. Sunbathing is important, especially this time of year,
and you can never lose a body or turn into anything you weren't already.

CRAYFISH WATCH THE MOON FALL

a
few
million years
pass ,

    then ,
    watch mantle
    begin descent

    into sea foam , &
    soft earth ,

        arms of seashore reach out , to
        help water help glass break fall ,

        soft pull , curved hands   here
        match crater , &   there   catch mountain .

then ,   (maria to maria)

ocean comes
up to ask ,
    " where've
they
    gone ? "

" who ? "

" you , moon ,
once with body like   gloss ,
bright wetness ,
young in this sky . "

" tell me , " ocean says ,
" what colour was it ?
how deep ? how warm ?
who lived in you ?
how long have they been gone — "

" grey is grey , "

moon answers .

"& time takes most things . "

I AM OFF TO MEET THE HIMALAYAS

[Himalaya, from Sanskrit: *himá* ("snow") + *ā-laya* ("dwelling")]

teeth fall yellow
from an old man's mouth .
cheeks bulging with time ,
unsalted . lips cross-stitched .
there is karmic —
& there is bowed —
held taunt in the hands
of men with burlap
sacks for bones ,
rivers for
eyes .

i met two rivers
on a slope ,
two arms lifted .
now i ask the dawn
to please them .
left with a seed buried
under a mountain .
two lilies
gutted the sky
for some water .
petals plump –
edges crisp –

the clouds
warmed .

over the sun
is some new relief .
that horizon is sweet —
unknowing —
prosperous .

A ROSE IS A MOUTH WITH NO TEETH

I ask you how many horizons you believe in.

You say two. One behind your teeth. One behind the sun.

I meet you where your hot neck ends. Where it entwines with daffodils and thick red vines.

You undo your tongue from your mouth and pass it to me like a spare key. I treasure the wetness that hangs from it like dewdrops. Clings to pink flesh. I treasure the way your saliva links wetly between our hands.

I know you had a name once. Something like Europa or Maha, something with an old vowel to bloat in your chest and hang like a drum. I know you had a name once but now naming seems reckless.

There are a thousand songs left to sing. Every name is a song. I don't know where a song goes once it is sung. I think a voice is a soul. I don't know how the throat can be ripe for that.

There is laughter pealing, a yellow bell. There are gulls who cry, an ocean above. The hum in your chest, unfurling. Try speaking this into an oyster sometime. Salt staining fat. Take both my lips if you want.

The best I can hope for is that this passes through you once, softly.

WE DON'T WANT TO LOVE PEOPLE SO DIFFERENT FROM US

I want to eat fruit the same way you eat fruit with your lips not your
teeth tongues stained with juice when I smile I want you to smile back
wipe the corner of my mouth with your thumb kiss me kiss your thumb
show me how fruit tastes in your mouth just a touch different from how
it tastes in mine

THE VERY SLOW STEPS TOWARD YOU

are not what my feet do.   There
are moments here.   Where
I remember what your hands   look like
when you hold them   out to me as we
laugh   & how   your eyes crease
like my palms.   Your eyes crease
like my palms & when I laugh   I can
taste blood in my cheeks.   What I am
saying is   we are speaking.
What I am trying to say   is   I speak
full of laughter   around you.   You make
my heart feel louder.   You make my   full
laughing heart feel louder.   Louder is under
my throat,   or under my tongue.   You
are both.   Soft to speak.   Even softer to
swallow.   I have had a hard time   before
swallowing things.   Now I am   singing to
the swallows resting   under my chest.   You make
me feel like   there is singing.   They are singing.

I AM LISTENING TO THE DOVES COO

who dropped
these petals?

"Allah miya has given you such nice hands to write with —
    such a nice mind — to write from — "

"This is where I write from." I grab my throat. "Here. *Here.*"

WHY I PRAY

[Islam, from Arabic: (s-l-m) "submission, reconciliation, surrender"]

I tap my knees on the ground twice , &
close my eyes (even though they've told me
not to) , & the thick fall of my hair has come
undone under my dupatta , & I can't tell
where is cloth & where is curl , & there are
dreams here under my knees , under this wood ,
beneath this house , & the house built behind it .

I ask my father why he taps his knees ,
& he says "not sure , " he says
" I love those dreams even if
I don't understand them , "
& understands what (after all)
but some kind of healing .

then I ask my mother , driving to
Nani's house , & she turns her answer
to the paddy fields , & confesses
" I will never find this kind
of forgiveness anywhere else — "
& forgiveness for what (after all)
but some kind of healing .

one evening , they ask me to recite
a few words of it in the garden ,
under the ash tree & the red mountains ,
& my knees shatter in their sockets ,
& my hair falls from its root ,
because I say " no ,
prayer is not a memory ,
prayer is a question . "

they smile , put my bones back together ,
sew my hair to my scalp , tuck a
curl behind my ear , & say
" asking for what (after all)
but some kind of healing . "

YOUR DEPARTURE, A LONELINESS

I pray best when my parents are getting on long-haul flights. I wake up wondering if I have the courage to be alone with my body again, or my cat. My mother hates my cat usually but today she's standing in the hallway before we leave, tying her shoes and petting the cat, saying, "Don't make a mess — stay off the couch — take care of her for me."

She doesn't see me, listening in the doorway. My father adores my cat. He talks to her all the time but decides not to even look at her the entire day before they leave. This is, truthfully, quite typical of how he loves. My mother's cheeks are red under the elevator lights so I ask her if she stole the lipstick that I stole from my sister. She says, "No — me chu thyouth pehran," and I ask, "Pehran what?' and she says, "You."

I try not to cry all day but it's especially hard in the car, under the engine's hum and cover of mostly dark. I avoid blinking. I tilt my face up. I don't really know why I'm doing this. Habit, shame or fear. I am worried about my father so I pester him all day, in my bossiest voice, about his medicine, his driving, his passport, his prayers. All the things I know he knows better than me. I don't ask for a hug but I ask at least ten times, "Are you sure you don't want me to park? — four suitcases is too much for two of you — ten dollars isn't that much," but they say, "No — don't worry — we'll be fine." We hug and I try to press into their bodies every word I cannot say. *I will miss you so much — it's hard to live together — but I want you to come back soon.*

On my way home, I listen to Joni Mitchell, which is a mistake. As I pull out the clicker that opens the garage, I remember how my dad always takes it out for me when he's sitting in the front seat and how my mother always put her hand on my shoulder when I park. So I park and I sit, for twenty minutes, finally crying — thinking about what it means to be alone, alone — feeling like a fool.

I REMEMBER AN INCIDENT WHERE MY MOTHER BEGS ME

not to turn out like my siblings and there was a time
none of them spoke English and I didn't realize that
until one day I turned to Papa and asked what language
echoed inside his head. There was a chicken factory
my mother and father both worked at by the lake
and I only asked about it when I started working
at the burger shop down the street. My father tells me
how he would work his business in the mornings and
go to the factory noon to midnight. He left

when the business picked up but this was where we
had Education and Opportunity so they spent their youth
years apart, my mother and father, they spent thirteen years
a part, two months here, three months there. When I was three,
I pushed my father out of bed and asked him who he was. Now
I'm twenty-three and they ask me who I am, try to understand
the ideas that have grown inside my head, ideas that don't translate
well, but I'm young and foolish, so I think I'm the only one
living between languages. I don't remember the time

we had to live in a storage unit or when my sister's
Halloween costume was made out of a garbage bag
and sometimes when you realize all your parents have lived
through you have nowhere to look but that one time
my mother left the house, overwhelmed and alone,
fighting with two teenagers, took a walk by the lake
and didn't come home until it was past dark. I waited

by the door until she came back. I burst into an anger
not meant for the body of a six-year-old. I held her
in my small arms as she begged me not to turn out
like them, like them, like who? I asked but I couldn't
tell if it was my siblings or something else and it was
something else because weeks later I found
a crumpled up church flyer in her coat pocket.

See, 9/11 just happened and our sweet Canadian,
church-going neighbours were handing out flyers
asking to evict every Muslim in the neighbourhood
and my mother had just fought with her changing
children and finished a shift at that horrible chicken
factory when they asked her to go back, go home,
go back to where you came from, and I imagine
she couldn't have found the words in any language
for the longing in her chest.

CHILDREN CACKLE LIKE A BAND OF HYENAS

and I see an icicle shaped like a sabre. I remember the sabre-toothed
tiger is extinct but could eat elephants and rhinos and bears. I remember
a cat is not a cat but a lineage. Humans are like that too, have lineage.
Ancestors. Shrouds we might return to and respect, if we wanted to,
if we remembered. But those shrouds are like this icicle and the children
laughing behind it. Tucked below gravel, held together by cold air.
I am under the train pulling into the station. There is a loose muscle
in my mouth I worry I might swallow. I am perpetually straining my jaw,
carefully holding my teeth apart. I wonder if I could grow canines like
the sabre-tooth, if I could ask that of my mouth. My mouth has asked
so many things of me. A news anchor moves his mouth in the shape of
WE ARE ALL DYING but the subtitles read BACK AT 6.
I am reminded that a mouth is just one way to wear a body, a vessel
that won't fit. Teeth are just one way to wear bone. There is always
a new name for reckoning but reckoning never changes. A tiger is
a tiger, whether the shape of its face or the size of its enemies
has changed. An empire is always an empire whether it holds your face
to the ground or lifts you up to touch the sky. I learned about the sabre-
toothed tiger without an age, as a child, when I pulled back my lips
and pressed my thumbs into my canines until I bled. My niece and
nephew ask me, *Is this fun?* like, *Are you listening?* and I am
grateful for small cacophonies. For the chance of renewal. For new
centuries to pass down in blood. To hope they might choose
better names for better empires.

ASIFA

I want to knock on the door of the temple where they trapped you. I want
to knock and knock again and have no one answer. I want to stand there
until my knuckles are swollen. Until my hands fall off. I want to call this
penance.

I have dreams of you that will not leave me. I imagine a purple shirt with
yellow flowers — two pigtails — and I wake up in a cold sweat. I have a
niece your age. I have four walking hearts. Two eyes. I cannot look at the
pictures left of you.

There are so many mountains in this place. It is not enough. There is
land enough to bury a thousand men and still. It is not enough. What
happened to you happened here.

I keep reading. Stories, memoirs, old rumours. Neatly written articles.
I take a hammer to the desk, the book, the page. I don't know the
difference between what I believe and what I don't want to know.

I dream I cut eight men down. I split them in half with my bare hands.
I don't see their faces or learn their names but I am pleased. I shake their
dirty blood off my wrists and spit out their bones. I call this a tree festival.
I know we are all Muslim here, but, in those dreams, I am a deranged and
beautiful god.

I dig a small grave for you, mark it in the northwest corner of the province. I don't know where the real one is. What remained of you was small, small already because you were. I don't think I deserve to visit your grave. I don't think anyone does and I hate myself for this.

I leave two halves of a lily in the dugout. I could set this entire valley on fire and it would never be enough. I watch a hawk scream in the sky and I know there is no way to go to sleep.

MIND'S EYE

who is the hawk
crying for

      who is the dragon
      guarding my memory

         who is the memory
         of being a child

            who is
            the echo

     who is the animal in the water
     pretending to be the water

     who is the bird in the sky
     acting like the sky

        who is
        screaming

    who is on fire
    but a sound

who is the hawk that eats
from my memories

     who is the desire
     to remember

     who is the horizon
     for hearing

        who is carrying the azan
        behind my ears

who is the mouth
that breathes it

who is the fire
behind your heart

who is the flower
behind the echo

who is louder
than the sun

IV.
Distances

holy. If I must be holy, let me make poems. If I must make poems, let
them be mouthed. If I must mouth anything, let it be worship. If I must
worship anything, let it be body. If I must be a body, let it be holy. If I
must be holy, let me make poems. If I must make poems, let them be
mouthed. If I must mouth anything, let it be worship. If I must worship
anything, let it be body. If I must be a body, let it be holy. If I must be
holy, let me make poems. If I must make poems, let them be mouthed. If
I must mouth anything, let it be worship. If I must worship anything, let it
be body. If I must be a body, let it be holy. If I must be holy, let me make
poems. If I must make poems, let them be mouthed. If I must mouth
anything, let it be worship. If I must worship anything, let it be body. If I
must be a body, let it be holy. If I must be holy, let me make poems. If I
must make poems, let them be mouthed. If I must mouth anything, let it
be worship. If I must worship anything, let it be body. If I must be a body,
let it be holy. If I must be holy, let me make poems. If I must make
poems, let them be mouthed. If I must mouth anything, let it be worship.
If I must worship anything, let it be body. If I must be a body, let it be
holy. If I must be holy, let me make poems. If I must make poems, let
them be mouthed. If I must mouth anything, let it be worship. If I must
worship anything, let it be body. If I must be a body, let it be holy. If I

DIRECTION, *after Claudia Rankine*

[73]

Longing, we say, because desire is full
of endless distances.

—Robert Hass

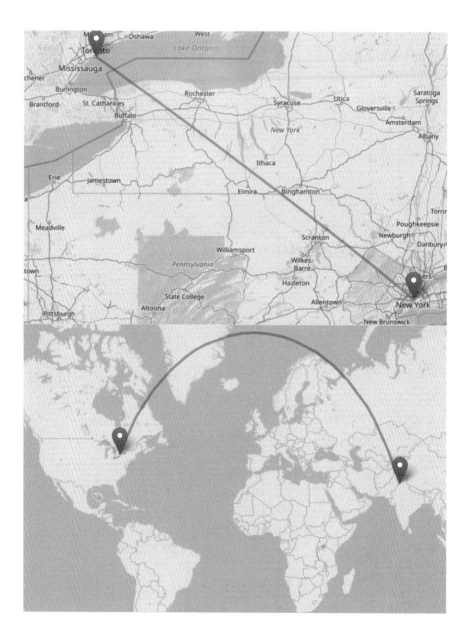

winter

We meet at a coffee shop. So much time has passed and who is time? Who is waiting by the windowsill? Maya and I make plans to go to a museum but we go to a bookshop instead. We're leaning in, learning how to talk to each other again. I say, *I'm obsessed with my grief* and she says, *I'm always in mourning.* She laughs and it's an extension of her body. She laughs and it moves the whole room. I say, *My home is an extension of my body* and she says, *Most days are better with a long walk.* The world moves without us — so we tend to a garden, a graveyard, a pot on the windowsill. Death is a comfort because it says, *Transform but don't hurry.* There is a tenderness to growing older and we are listening for it. Steadier ways to move through the world and we are learning them. A way to touch your own body. A touch that says, *Dig deeper.* There, in the ground, there is our memory. I am near enough my roots. Time is my friend. Tomorrow is a place we are together.

Across the world, my mother watches the gardener across the street play with his children. My parents and I have walked by the same trees but never together. Scattered, we wait for spring. We share the sun. A walk is the chance to stop by the bridge, to see if the stream will say anything new. Each step, a hope, closing the gap between seasons. Fall where we are together. I ask Francis, *What are your intentions?* like, *What are you reaching for?* In the oldest language we know, intention means *to stretch.* I am looking for a map. Something to mould touch. *If I know how to call for you, you will come near me.* This is what my hope says. Sometimes I forget that hope is not the worst of my duties. That lovelessness and loneliness are not the same. When I am alone, I am lucky to watch the trees turn green. When I am hungry, I am glad to hear your voice. Beneath my voice is a promise — *I want to take you on my walk.* I want to listen with you for whatever makes anything new.

Manahil, in the word *surrender,* there is a love poem. It says, *I have been looking for you in the grass.* The grass is a place I call my hands. Memory is a city of moss, a circle of dew. My hands are heavy, soaked in time. Any question lights up my body with sound. Time is a place that bends. I have so many questions. Let's start with — *What do you know about the moon? Is the moon another word for my god? What about all my gods behind it?* My God is a lineage of light. A longing. My God says, *I want to hold your hand.* I want to feel small in front of an ocean with you.

Standing in front of a field full of dandelions, I cannot help but think of you. This annoys me. There goes the sun, wandering by. Here is the world where my eyes drank you in. Here is the world where, if my eyes drink enough light, everything changes colour. Look at that cloud. I could put you in its shape. There is nothing I could point to and not find you in. Sometimes this gives me a headache. For now, yellow dots green until the grass is one big speckled fish. *What are we swimming toward?* I want to ask the wind. No answer but the wildflower sprouting earnestly by the trash can. Listen, Yasmin. Someday, I will stand in front of a field again. The grass will be frail — late summer — too much sun. But I will still thirst for light. So if I find even one yellow blossom peeking out of that dust, I will think, *Oh — you.* And it will still be you.

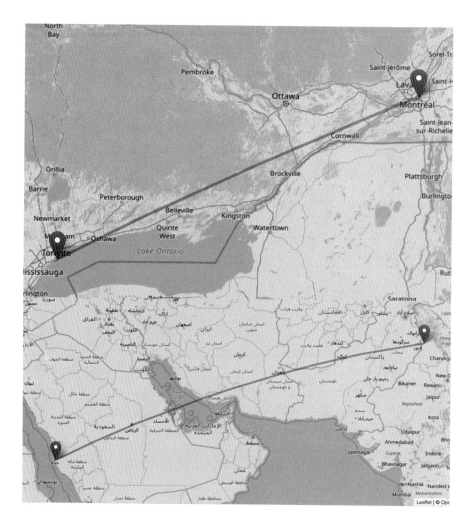

spring

I would start my explanation with, *In every memory I have of you, you have a look of patience on your face.* I know how you love your family. I know there is no real question here to begin with, just knots of time neither of us can untangle. We shouldn't have to. Yes, I know we have tried. Yes, I know we have the courage. But lately, Tabir, when I dream of you, you ask me if you are a coward. I know the answer but the explanation would take years. With time, this will become easier to hold because grief is good to us both. Grief says, *I hope summer is kinder* because grief knows you deserve kindness. Grief weeps when the world does not give it to you. This kind of love is not out of use. Grief is not a useful thing to begin with and neither am I — so here we are, mourning our whole lives. Let's marvel at our tenacity. We knew from the start. This did not dissuade us. Something inside you said, *Reach for the world* and you did. There is nothing to do now but run our hands under cold water. No, I am not sorry either. Sorrow is a promise I make without sense. It sounds like a prayer. It circles my memory.

I wake up two hours earlier than I'm supposed to — my stomach hurts. Acid on the street. On the sidewalk, in the air, there is your nose. The space between *your* and *my* burns. Constantly shrinking. That's what acid does. Always tries to get away from itself. Is that restoration? This city wasn't built for me. This city wasn't built. This city is old, low to the ground, full of hills. On Saturday, it will snow. I will lay down among bales of hay and my life will drive by. On Friday, I will drive. Prayer is not obligatory for travellers because God knows they will do it anyway. I drink from my worry, a callous, my tongue. Where else would I find God? On the road because the road is endless. My worry is endless. I wish God was too but God is made of ends. My hands are the end of me. I offer them to God like *Here, here I am, I understand you.* My worry does not understand me. My worry is not a prayer. It trusts no one, especially not my God. It sings *run run run* inside me until I do. Until I'm gone.

Sometimes I am so angry with God, I want to wrestle. That's why there's myth, right? A thousand years ago, someone felt the same as me and now I live in that story's shadow. Time pulls our teeth apart. History climbs inside our mouth. God hands you a book and says, *Eat.* Who can forgive ambivalence? Your lip was bleeding. God was wearing the face of my father, distant and empty. Twilight filled the room. History left with silence, the door undone. *God gives and takes with both hands,* my mother always says. My anger was made in that gap. Its obliterating hollow.

Twelve years later, the foundation is crumbling. You asked, *Why did you pay so much?* when you really meant, *How did you know you loved me?* Who were you asking? Love was something you were learning to beg for. Begging was nothing. Disgust was new. Now the spider crawls through your window and no one flinches. A ghost spits in your eye and your mother cries instead. It is artful to admit you knew no better. To bring your father to tears then apologize. To watch red-faced spirits wander your dreams and laugh. You did not know what was shaking in the bush but you knew better than to look. It's been twelve years but it's also been six. There are so many ways we can give ourselves to time. There is only so much of us passing through.

summer

How does a smile get inside you? There is the sky, tilted with light. There is the loosening we call a sunset. Here is where Natalina danced and here is where Alyson and I laughed. Lily shared a blanket until the ants came crawling. We didn't mind because we understood hunger. Open your mouth and I am full of oxygen again. Love is what is alive between us as good as air. Behind me now is a sky full of colour. Beneath my face is a soreness — smile marking muscle. When I am old, you will sit on my skin. The corners of my mouth. Joy is a promise we make with our body. My skin like the sky is bright with memory. I am always falling apart and back together again. There is always more sky to drive toward. New light to cling to.

Two days ago, I saw you in a dream. You were under some bridge. Then the sky stopped to ask, *Do angels have ears?* How should I know who can carry light? Look at that moth, breathing with its wings. At the window, there was a congregation. I was sleeping. Yes, someone was waiting to speak. I had left a light on. Yes, birds have that habit. Do you understand? My mother has never let me kill a moth. She says, *Take it outside* and I do. I release it into the night, or it, the night, into me. If I could speak to the sky, I would say, *I know you are just a bridge.* The angels might be listening. In my dream, you became the moon. You asked, *Who do you see in my face?* The night stole my answer.

I tell Harrison, *The way the mountains touch the clouds makes the sky feel closer.* My family is always trying to touch the sky. My niece's name means *bird of paradise* and she is. Her shoulders were so soft when she was born, both fit tucked inside my palm. I ask her, *What do you think is up there?* and she tells me stories of storms that weep and wander, a hush that follows the wind. I have been wandering. On the phone, my mother says, *Ajao abh hamare paas bhi* and I want to say, *All my life all I've wanted is to be close to you.* Instead, I tell her about whales — why they live to become grand-mothers, how they play and grieve. I ask Minelle, *What is joy?* like, *What is sacred?* and she says, *The butterfly on the window.* It is the fourth anniversary of her mother's death and she is learning how to feel close to her again. Her name means *a wish come true* and she is. There is a wish that has been following me across the fields of my life. I feel it tap my shoulder in front of Harrison, in the sunlight that follows me at breakfast with Minelle, the ache in my hands when I pull a card for jaye. Page of Wands. I have told three friends in three days, *Slow down.* There are mountains inside us we are still learning to climb. Rivers that stretch and settle across our shoulders. We are the valley, a mouth turned toward the sky. Someday, I want to embrace a child and offer them my name. I want to say, *This is the world I want to love you in.* My beloveds are building the places I want you to meet. Memory is not an easy inheritance but it loves joy, follows grief. I don't know which horizon leads to you but I am looking for it. I don't know where the mountains end but I am on my way to you.

This is what I wish my dreams were like, Karenveer says and we are sitting on two chairs in front of the sky. She says, *When you lose that person, something vanishes.* A home becomes a house. A roof, a chair, somewhere no one sits anymore. Time is slipping away, over my face, under your hands. Grief punctures a hole in time we slip through. We wait. Weep. Wander. Wonder about her face in your dreams. Ask, *Whose dream?* like, *Was that really her?* Only the crow knows. The crow, who knows how to laugh and recognize a face. Wisdom passes mouth to mouth. *When a crow caws, family is coming home.* There is still someone who calls you home.

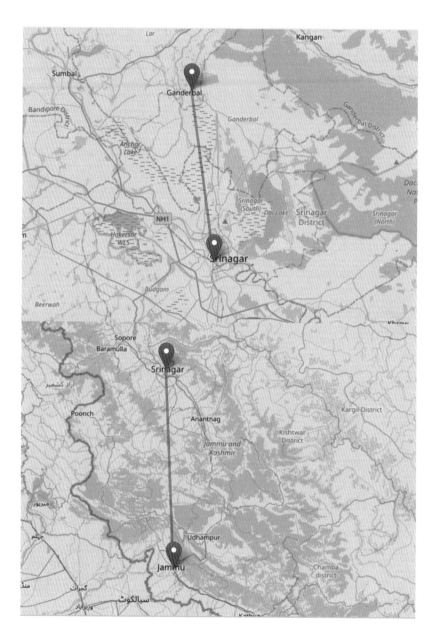

fall

Today I eat eggs. The roses in the garden grow taller than me, reaching for the sun. I do not drink coffee. I crave it but it does not hurt me to drink ginger tea instead. I am not tired. The stray kittens keep trying to get inside the house and my father says, *Let them.* Their little brown noses in our laundry, under the dining table, in the kitchen drawers. There are so many sun-warmed spots to sit. I have a desk. I put aloe vera in the drawers for when my hands and lips get dry as I work. I work. I watch two flowers bloom. I guess their names. The kittens are not afraid of wasps. Their mother finally trusts me. I do not pluck a single hair from my face. I make goals and fail and make more. I watch the sunset from the attic window. My father sits in the light. My hair smooths to two curtains down the sides of my face. Even the wood whispers, *I love you.*

If I am lost, I have enough buttons. A stranger says, *You look so lovely in that phiran.* That velvet suits your skin. The colour yellow beckons me. If I am, then I am lost. If I am lost, someone will take me home. Feet make a mark in the grass. A path licks its way into the dirt and now there's an echo. I walked high enough up the mountain for light to look like smoke and even when no one knew each other, we made a point to greet each other like family. *Family* is another word for this place. For the place it makes of us.

I have gone long nights with the mouth of sorrow at my throat and only whispered to you in the dark. Nana, in my dreams, I am running. I am always running. I could be, I mean. *Never* is a word I want to claw out of the world but can't. Not yet. Not while I am tied to the post of my bed, the stake of my body, glowing in the dark. Nothing I do asks anything of the world except, *Listen.* My hands are a plea. *Dear God,* my hands weep — what do we do now? God reaches through my hands, heart wound in light. At the end of God's hands, someone is waiting for me. Someone is holding a lilac, or lily. It depends on the day. The memory climbing out of you, or in. Something grows and grows again. You kiss my dreams, the only answer.

I follow a song to my room. The clothes I left piled on the chair are folded. A bowl of cut fruit on the desk. A voice floats in through the open window. *Zindagi aur kuch bhi nahi teri meri kahani hai / Ek pyar ka nagma hai.* A moment that has not happened yet — my mother walking with a cane, tired hands, grey hair, back bent. My mother who begins to look more and more like her own. My mother who sat across from me, kissed me so many times with her eyes, and said, *You are my daughter.* You look just like me today.

NOTES

I.

"Dorsal" is written after Mitski's song "Pink in the Night" from *Be the Cowboy* (Dead Oceans, 2018).

The epigraph of this section is from "Cienaños de un pueblo" by Gabriel García Márquez in *Visión* (July 1967) but which I discovered through Centro Gabo's article "La amistaden 14 reflexiones de Gabriel García Márquez" (August 2018) and translated myself.

"Masha'Allah" is written after Danusha Laméris's poem "Insha'Allah" from *The Moons of August* (Autumn House Press, 2014).

The epigraph of "Today and Every Day, Without You" is from Aleksandar Ristović's poem "Day-dreaming in Midst of Spring Labors" in *Devil's Lunch* (Faber & Faber, 1999), translated by Charles Simic, but which I discovered as the epigraph of Heather Christle's *The Trees The Trees* (Octopus Books, 2011).

The epigraph of "Memory Is Sleeping" is from Billy-Ray Belcourt's memoir *A History of My Brief Body* (Penguin Canada, 2020).

"Bilabial" is written in conversation with Myung Mi Kim's *Commons* (University of California Press, 2002) and would not exist if not for the Poetry/Race/Form workshop facilitated by Zoe Imani Sharpe and Fan Wu.

"How Many Languages Make a Tongue?" is written after Yoko Tawada's poem "Hamlet No See" published in lyrikline.

"Tragedy" is written after Alejandra Pizarnik's poem "The Awakening" from *Extracting the Stone of Madness: Poems 1962–1972* (New Directions, 2016), translated by Yvette Siegert.

"Princess Mononoke (1997)" is written as ekphrasis after the eponymous movie directed by Hayao Miyazaki and produced by Studio Ghibli.

"Meditation" would not exist if not for Aisha Sasha John's workshop Poetry Is Prayer hosted by The Poetry Project.

"Between Spring Equinox and Summer Solstice, Tonight" is written after Emily Jungmin Yoon's poem "Between Autumn Equinox and Winter Solstice, Today" from *A Cruelty Special to Our Species* (Ecco Press, 2018). It also quotes Agha Shahid Ali's poem "Stationary" from *The Half-Inch Himalayas* (Wesleyan University Press, 1987) and makes reference to *Call Me Ishmael Tonight: A Book of Ghazals* (W. W. Norton, 2003).

"Sing" is written after Juan Felipe Herrera's poem "Social Distancing," designed by Anthony Cody and published by the Academy of American Poets on Poets.org in April 2020.

II. Forming Glory

"Relief" is written after a common translation of Rumi's poem "I said: what about my eyes?"

All of the poems in this section are erasures of German Orientalist scholar Josef van Ess's lecture "The Youthful God. Anthropomorphism in Early Islam" delivered in 1988 at Arizona State University as the University Lecture in Religion and published in *Kleine Schriften* (Brill, 2018) edited by Hinrich Biesterfeldt.

The first epigraph is from M. NourbeSe Philip's "Interview with an Empire" in *Lemon Hound,* excerpted from *Blank: Essays and Interviews by M. NourbeSe Philip* (Book*hug Press, 2017).

The second epigraph is from a common translation of Rabia of Basra's poem, "Die Before You Die."

III.

"Reaching" is written after Anne Carson's poem "The Glass Essay" from *Glass, Irony, and God* (New Directions, 1995).

The epigraph of this section is from Alex Dimitrov's poem "Love" from *Love and Other Poems* (Copper Canyon Press, 2021).

The transliterated Kashmiri in "Your Departure, A Loneliness" translates to "I am so (full of) longing" and "Longing what?"

"Asifa" is written in mourning of the kidnapping, rape, and murder of an eight-year-old Bakarwal girl, Asifa Bano, in the Rasana village near Kathua, Jammu.

IV. Distances

"Direction" is written after Claudia Rankine's interview "The History Behind the Feeling" with Aaron Coleman in *The Spectacle.*

The epigraph of this section is from Robert Hass's poem "Meditation at Lagunitas" from *Praise* (Ecco Press, 1979) but which I discovered first as the epigraph of Leila Chatti's poem "Fasting in Tunis" in *Tunsiya/ Amrikiya* (Bull City Press, 2018).

The maps in this section were all created on distancefromto.net using OpenStreetMaps. The maps in "winter" indicate the distance from New York City to Toronto and Mississauga to Amritsar; in "spring," Toronto to Montréal and Amritsar to Jeddah; in "summer," Whitby to Mississauga and Vancouver to Brampton; in "fall," Srinagar to Ganderbal and Jammu to Srinagar.

The transliterated Urdu in "There is a wish" translates to "Come closer to us now too."

The transliterated Hindi in "I follow a song" are lyrics from the song "Ek Pyar Ka Nagma Hai," written by Santosh Anand and sung by Lata Mangeshkar and Mukesh in the movie *Shor* (dir. Manoj Kumar, 1972). The lyrics translate to "Life is no more than our story / One song of love."

ACKNOWLEDGEMENTS

Thank you to the editors and staff of the following journals, anthologies, and periodicals for publishing earlier versions of poems in this collection:

Arc Poetry Magazine: "Masha'Allah"
Best Canadian Poetry 2020: "Why I Pray"
Canthius: "Why I Pray"
Flypaper Lit: "Dorsal" and "Direction"
Glass: "Asifa"
Half a Grapefruit Magazine: "We Don't Want to Love People So Different from Us" and "We Are Whispering in the Dark"
Hayden's Ferry Review: "Between Spring Equinox and Summer Solstice, Tonight"
In the Mood: "Princess Mononoke (1997)"
Islam in the City: "Children Cackle like a Band of Hyenas"
LooseLeaf Magazine: "I Remember an Incident Where My Mother Begs Me"
The Margins: "Relief" and "Tragedy"
Nuance: "Schizotheism"
Peach Mag: "A Rose Is a Mouth with No Teeth"
Poem-a-Day: "Tomorrow is a place"
Poetry Daily: "Memory Is Sleeping"
The Puritan: "Memory Is Sleeping" and "I Am Off to Meet the Himalayas"
Room: "Meditation" and "Reaching"
Savant-Garde: "Good Morning, the Sun in October"
The Strand: "How Many Languages Make a Tongue?"

Thank you to everyone at House of Anansi Press, especially Kevin Connolly. Thank you to the Ontario Arts Council and the Canada Council of Arts. Thank you to the Institute of Islamic Studies at the University of Toronto, especially Anver Emon and Nambogga Sewali, for the opportunity to transform a previous version of "Forming Glory" into a display piece for the office. Thank you to Amira Mittermaier, without whom writing "Forming Glory" would have not been possible. Thank you to the Banff Centre for the Arts for the chance to experience the 2019 Emerging Writers Intensive and to Aaron, Canisia, Chim, Cooper, Leslie, Lou, jaye, Natasha, and Nicole for the kindness and the ruckus.

Thank you to the places that made this book possible. My home near the Missinnihe river and in Tkaronto, land stewarded since time immemorial by the Mississaugas of the Credit, the Anishinabeg, the Chippewa, the Wendat, and the Haudenosaunee among many other diverse First Nations, Métis, and Inuit peoples. My home under the Zabarwan mountains and in Kashmir, land shared by the Pahari, Gujri, Bakarwal, Ladakhi, Shina, Balti, and Hunza peoples among others.

Thank you to the people who make me possible. Thank you to my friends, named and unnamed, past and present. Ahmed. Cleo and Terry. Em. Francis and Andrew. Harrison. Lily, Natalina, and Alyson. Marloes. Manahil, Hamzah, and Roha. Sav. Shawk. Your love is my favourite poem. Thank you to my mentors and role models, teachers who became friends. Eduardo and Fati. Jairan and Nada. Ralph and Tami. You listened and cared and changed my life. Thank you to my family. Mama, Papa, Anna Baji, and Samer Bhaiya. Nana, Nani, Dadu, Dadi, and Phopho. Humnah, Hadi, Lyla, and Hani. Tabir and Zehra. I am yours first. I love you very much.

And thank you — you, here, with me on this page. Thank you for bringing these words to life.

Author photograph: Hamzah Amin

SANNA WANI loves daisies. She lives in Mississauga, Ontario, and Srinagar, Kashmir. This is her first collection of poetry.